A Study of Prayer and Praying

Chad Sychtysz

© 2024 Spiritbuilding Publishers.
All rights reserved. No part of this book may be reproduced in any form without the written permission of the publisher.

Published by
Spiritbuilding Publishers
9700 Ferry Road, Waynesville, Ohio 45068

A STUDY OF PRAYER AND PRAYING
By Chad Sychtysz

ISBN: 978–1955285–92–6

Spiritbuilding
PUBLISHERS

spiritbuilding.com

Table of Contents

Introductory Comments 1

What Is Prayer? 3

The Objective of Prayer 7

Prayer Is Protection from the Enemy 9

Does God Really Hear Our Prayers? 11

The Mechanics of Prayer 17

The Lord's Instructions on Prayer 21

What to Pray For 26

General Topics of Prayer 29

Final Thoughts 35

Article: "Intimacy with God" 36

Article: "Having a Thirst for God" 38

Article: "We Have an Advocate" 40

Article: "In His Time" 42

Article: "Holding On and Letting Go" 44

Article: "Praying for One Another" 46

Article: "Giving Thanks" 48

Sources Used for This Study 51

Cover design by Larissa Lynch

Introductory Comments

- Someone has said, "Prayer is our lifeline to God." This helps us to understand its importance: if you are floundering in the ocean and someone throws you a lifeline, you will cling to it as though your life depended upon it—for it most certainly will. So it is with prayer: your soul's forgiveness, health, and survival (especially into the world to come) depends upon this lifeline called "prayer." It is not really *your* lifeline to God, but *His* lifeline to you. Without it, you will drown in the sea of darkness and moral confusion, along with the rest of the unbelieving and unconverted world. You cannot afford to end that way; you do not *have* to end that way.
  - The positive benefits of prayer are innumerable. God "is able to do far more abundantly beyond all that we ask or think" (Eph. 3:20)—He can perform *better* than we can ask, know, or expect of Him. We offer prayers in faith, hoping that God knows what He is doing, can deliver on His promises, and will protect us from spiritual ruin. And "God is faithful" (1 Cor. 1:9) to honor our trust in Him: He has proved it over the several thousand years covered in Scripture.
  - Thus, when we pray to God, we are not simply crossing our fingers in desperate hope that He will hear our prayers and answer them intelligently. On the contrary, He promises to *exceed* our requests in ways that we would never expect. Think of the confidence expressed by the psalmist in Psalm 116:1–2: "I love the Lord because He hears My voice and my supplications. Because He has inclined His ear to me, therefore I shall call upon Him as long as I live." This should be our view toward our own prayers to God: He *inclines His ear* to us—the Creator of the universe knows who we are and listens to our prayers!

- Why a study on prayer is always needed:
  - Christians are being assaulted with secular and wicked influences every day. We need not only to react to this assault, but we must take proactive steps against allowing it to destroy us. The fact is: *any Christian will be overcome by the world* who does not devote himself to a meaningful prayer life.

- Christians are to be "devoted to prayer"—this takes time, training, and work. You will not be "devoted" during a Bible class, sermon, or church service—or in a week, month, or year. Being devoted to prayer is a vocation, not a project; it is a lifestyle, not an event.
- God wants you to communicate with Him—and you need to know *how* to do so. He *teaches* you how to do so through His revealed word. It is His responsibility to have provided that teaching. It is *your* responsibility to submit to it, practice it, and "excel still more" in it (1 Thess. 4:1).
- Even if you are already good at praying, there is always room for improvement. None of us has mastered the work of prayer, although some may certainly be much further ahead than others. Prayer is not something that we isolate or target as a specific work that needs to be done (separate from all other Christian work). Rather, it is a part of *all* we do in service for God. No work for the Lord is complete apart from prayer. The better we understand and practice prayer, the better our service will be in God's kingdom.
- Not only this, but better (more thoughtful, meaningful, and personal) prayers lead us into deeper communion with God through Christ. God wants us to "draw near" to Him (James 4:8), and this is only possible through the avenue of prayer.

❑ What is strongly suggested:
- Pray to God 10 minutes every morning or every evening for the duration of this class: this is in addition to whatever time for prayer you are currently using.
- Take a mental "snapshot" of where you are right now and see if it does not improve—possibly in ways you did not expect—by the end of this study.

What Is Prayer?

Prayer is not a rabbit's foot or any other form of a "good luck" charm. It is not an amulet which grants special powers to the one who possesses it. It is not a magical incantation that only works if the right words are intoned in the right order. It is not a prying tool which forces God's hand to give a person what he wants. It is not a magic lamp, and God is not a genie. It is not a special coin, and God is not a dispensing machine. It is not a spiritual narcotic, designed only to offer therapeutic solace to the one praying, but accomplishing little else in the process. It is not a desperate, last-ditch effort of escaping one's personal ruin by invoking heavenly powers after that person's own attempts at salvation have failed miserably.[1]

- ❏ Three general kinds of prayer:

    - <u>Appeal</u> (for grace and forgiveness). This is related to the sin offerings in the Levitical sacrificial system of the Law of Moses (Lev. 4:1ff). While prayers are not blood offerings, they are necessary for atonement.

    - <u>Petition</u> (for things + consecration for service). This is related to the burnt offerings of the Law (Lev. 1:1ff). Burnt offerings were consecratory in nature, expressing a desire to draw near to God in holiness and fellowship.

    - <u>Praise to God</u> (Psalm 33:1, 147:1, and Heb. 13:15). This is related to the freewill or "peace" offerings of the Law (Lev. 3:1ff). Only one who is at peace with God can offer prayers of praise to Him. Such praise is offered *after* his sins have been atoned for (through grace and forgiveness) *and* he has consecrated himself to the Lord's service (a promise to draw near to God).

- ❏ Prayer must be viewed as a *sacrifice* that "costs" us something (2 Sam. 24:24)

---

[1] Chad Sychtysz, *Seeking the Sacred* (Waynesville, OH: Spiritbuilding Publishers, 2009), 230.

- This "cost" may be time, convenience, our forgiveness, the respect of non–believers (who ridicule us), something we need to let go of (for the sake of repentance), etc.
- See Mark 11:25, Luke 18:9–12, Eph. 5:3–4, 1 Tim. 2:8, and James 1:6.

❑ Prayer is a *sacred form of communication with God*. It should never be treated as a casual ritual, forced obligation, or mere mechanical exercise.
- This implies the existence of **fellowship** with God. Whoever prays to God must believe that He exists and that fellowship with Him is real and powerful.
- This requires **faith** that God is worth "seeking" or pursuing (Heb. 11:6). Even though we cannot literally see God, the evidence of His existence and the effectiveness of praying to Him is also real and powerful.
- This involves **intimacy** (closeness) of His fellowship: it is necessary and achievable.

Please read "Intimacy with God" (page 36) and answer the following:

1.) Why is prayer considered "intimate" communication with God?

2.) In prayer, we fully reveal ourselves to God, but does He fully reveal (or *has* He fully revealed) Himself to *us*—or is this a one–sided disclosure?

3.) What does it take to develop intimacy (in prayer)? What are some incorrect ways that one might try to achieve this intimacy?

Please read "Having a Thirst for God" (page 38) and answer the following:

1.) Why is self–reliance of one's spiritual well–being incompatible with praying to God?

2.) Does praying *by itself* indicate a person's trust in God? Or are there other reasons for which someone might pray?

3.) Should we come to God hungry and thirsty? If so, what does this mean, exactly?

Prayer is the sacred means of communication which God has given us to use for our own good. Since He has given it to us (at no cost), it is a gift. Like all gifts which God gives to us, it is supposed to be appreciated, used wisely, and (thus) not misused. Prayer is a privilege, not a right. However, we are to respond rightly to the gift of prayer, just as we are to respond rightly to the gift of grace, the gift of mercy, the gift of forgiveness, and the many other gifts He gives to His children. This necessarily implies that one must be a child of God in order to receive this gift. We have no record of God responding to the prayers of those who are not interested in having a right relationship with Him. In fact, we see just the opposite in Scripture (see Isaiah 1:15–16, 59:1–2, John 9:31, and 1 Peter 3:7). God is not obligated to hear the prayers of those who refuse to surrender their hearts to Him. Those who pray to God only when they find themselves in a perilous predicament (but do not trust God otherwise) profane the sacredness of prayer. They have no appreciation for its intended purpose, just as they have no real appreciation for God Himself.[2]

- ❑ Prayer is:

    - A *gift* of grace—a privilege we do not deserve and cannot earn. All gifts of grace are conditional by nature: we are expected to be *prepared* to receive them. All such gifts are meant to be used in service to the God who gave them.

    - An *act* of worship (Eph. 3:14–21). We pay homage to God through our sacred communication with Him. For His part, God seeks those who will worship Him in prayer and in whatever other manner He has instructed us (John 4:23–24).

    - An *act* of faith (Heb. 11:6, James 1:5–8). We can only claim to *have* faith when we demonstrate acts *of* faith—acts which God has told us to perform in His name. Since "we walk by faith, not

---

2   Sychtysz, *Seeking the Sacred,* 203–204.

by sight" (2 Cor. 5:7), we do not pray only when we have factual confirmation of how these prayers will turn out (to be discussed later). Instead, we pray *in faith* that God will respond *and* will serve our best interest in His response.

- An *act* of confession (1 John 1:6–10): we confess that God exists, He is real and powerful, He hears our prayers, He acts on our prayers, and we are blessed and benefited by having prayed to Him. We *also* use prayer to confess our sins to God as a necessary precursor to receiving His forgiveness for those sins. For example:
  - The prayer of the Levites (Neh. 9:5–38)
  - The prayer of Daniel (Dan. 9:4–19)
  - The prayer of Isaiah (Isa. 63:7 – 64:12)

- An *outpouring* of joy or relief (Rev. 5:9–14). Prayer is not always about asking for things; it is also for expressing our joy, gratitude, and deep appreciation to God for all that He does for us. For example:
  - The prayer of Hannah (1 Sam. 2:1–10)
  - The prayer of Mary (Luke 1:46–55)
  - The prayer of the apostles (Acts 4:23–31)

- What Christians do naturally:
  - The early disciples (Acts 1:14)
  - The early Christians (Acts 2:42)
  - The apostles' devotion (Acts 6:4)
  - The example of Cornelius (Acts 10:2, 4)
  - The many examples of Paul (Eph. 3:14, Col. 1:9, 2 Thess. 1:11, 3:1, etc.)
  - The *Hebrews* writer's example (Heb. 13:18)
  - "With all prayer and petition pray at all times in the Spirit, and … be on the alert with all perseverance and petition for all the saints" (Eph. 6:18); "Be devoted to prayer" (Col. 4:2); "Pray without ceasing" (1 Thess. 5:17)

The Objective of Prayer

- ❑ What prayer does (and does not do):

  - Prayer is not intended to inform God of anything (Heb. 4:12–13). There is nothing that you can tell God that He does not already know fully and accurately.
  - Prayer is not intended to persuade God to accept our form of reasoning, etc.
  - Prayer is not intended merely to *get* things (James 4:1–3).
  - Prayer *is* a form of personal humility *and* absolute dependence upon God
    - "But seek first His kingdom and His righteousness, and all these things will be added to you" (Mat. 6:33)—prayer is a vital part of "seeking."
    - "Be anxious for nothing, but in everything by prayer and supplication with thanksgiving let your requests be made known to God" (Phil. 4:6)—prayer is necessary for dealing with anxiety (fear) and trials of faith.
    - "Humble yourselves…casting all your anxiety upon Him, because He cares for you" (1 Peter 5:6–7)—prayer is necessary for humility and trusting God.

- ❑ Prayer:

  - Keeps us focused upon godliness (1 Tim. 4:8–10).
  - Keeps us from becoming self-absorbed and unfocused (Mat. 16:23). God is not a God of confusion (1 Cor. 14:33) and wants us to keep our attention "fixed" on Him and His Son (1 Tim. 4:10, Heb. 12:2).
  - Keeps us from succumbing to powerful temptations or addictions (Col. 3:1–3). Such things always lead us away from God; prayer keeps us close to Him.
  - Is one of the three keys to a healthy Christian life (along with *study* and *fellowship*). These are not objectives in themselves but are necessary in pursuit of the main objective—a well-supplied and enduring faith.

- Serves as a witness of faith. When you pray in the presence of others, you proclaim what you believe to be real, true, and worth practicing.

❑ What Heb. 4:14–16 teaches us (among other things) that will enhance our prayer life:

- Jesus Christ is our "high priest"—one who intercedes for us (more than we know).
- He can "sympathize with our weaknesses"—He knows what it is like to be human.
- He "has been tempted in all things"—not with every *literal example* of temptation but every *form* or *nature* of it (1 John 2:16), beyond what we will ever face.
- Yet, He never *sinned*: He was subjected to temptation (like us) but never succumbed to it (unlike us); He has faced our same trials but never failed to be faithful to God.
- Therefore, we can "draw near with confidence to the throne of grace": we do not have to explain our situation or fear being misunderstood or unfairly judged.

Please read "We Have an Advocate" (page 40) and answer the following:

1.) How does "Jesus Christ the righteous" serve as our Advocate (1 John 2:1–2)? What does this have to do with prayer?

2.) Do we need legal representation, so to speak, to approach the throne of God? If not, why not? If so, is Jesus both necessary and qualified to provide this?

3.) Are there conditions required of us for Jesus to serve as our Advocate? If not, why not? If so, what are these?

Prayer Is Protection from the Enemy (Satan)

- ❑ Satan is a real, powerful, and destructive *adversary* to Christians everywhere. His strategy is to separate you from God **by attacking your prayer life.** Do you believe this?

- ❑ Satan's assault on your prayer life includes the following strategies:[3]

    - Devalue your prayers: diminish your hope, dull your desire, rob you of passion.
    - Attempt to disorient you, so that you focus on "fighting" vs. fighting against *Satan*.
    - Magnify and exploit your weaknesses to fill you with doubt rather than faith.
    - Constantly remind you of your past failures so you feel unforgiven and unforgivable.
    - Divide and destroy your marriage (and/or other meaningful relationships).
    - Undermine your commitment to Christ, making you compromise your integrity while still making you *feel* or *appear* "faithful," "spiritual," and "sincere" even when you are *not*.
    - Tempt you with sin, convincing you that you can practice sin without consequence.
        - Moral impurity weakens prayer and praying.
        - Moral purity strengthens prayer, which strengthens moral purity.

---

[3] The following list is adapted from Priscilla Shirer, *Fervent* (Nashville: B & H Publishing Group, 2015). I also strongly recommend my book, *This World Is Not Your Home* (Spiritbuilding Publishers, 2022), which gives considerable detail to Satan's world ("the darkness"), his "schemes," and what he does to mislead us.

- Bombard you with distractions, interferences, others' demands, etc. to enslave you to a schedule filled with unspiritual and unimportant "stuff" rather than allowing you to focus on your spiritual and *extremely important* relationship with God.
  - "Pressure" (which creates self–inflicted "stress") is a form of idolatry: we bow down to a false god of our own making vs. the God of heaven.
  - Contrast with Psalm 61:2–4, 62:1–2, 147:10–11, and Mat. 6:33.
- Attempt to fill your heart with anger, bitterness, and negativity—often, to keep you from being forbearing and forgiving (Col. 3:12–15).

- Attempt to disconnect you from Christians and "the church" to keep you isolated, out–of–touch, and removed from your moral responsibilities to God's people.

❑ Satan is an impostor: he wants you to think he has God–like power, but he does not.
  - He cannot create anything new; he only tweaks, maligns, and corrupts what exists.
  - He cannot read your mind (thoughts)—only a divine Being can do this (and Satan is not divine), but he *can* and *does* closely observe your habits and behavior.
  - He cannot destroy your soul or condemn your soul to hell (but *you* can).
  - He is the "father of lies" (John 8:44): anyone who lies—to God, himself, or others—imitates Satan rather than Christ (1 Cor. 11:1).
  - God cannot be destroyed but Satan can and will be destroyed, as will his followers.

Questions

1.) If we "submit ... to God" and "draw near to" Him, we can "resist the devil and he will flee from you" (James 4:7–8).

   a. But what if we do *not* submit to God or draw near to Him—can we still "resist the devil"? Can we ever resist the devil without God's help?

   b. What does prayer have to do with submitting and drawing near to God?

4.) Notice that much of what Satan does is distract us with lesser things rather than launch a full–scale attack on us. Why might petty distractions be far more effective in overcoming us than a direct attack?

Does God Really Hear Our Prayers?

- ❏ Whether God "hears" one's prayers *is* conditioned upon that person's moral fitness:

    - God will not listen to those who will not seek Him (John 9:31).
    - God will not listen to strangers (Mat. 7:21–23).
    - The prayers of a righteous man accomplish much (James 5:16); the prayers of an unrighteous man accomplish nothing (Isa. 1:15–17, in principle).
    - An improper attitude toward one's "fellow heir" can hinder prayers (1 Peter 3:7).

- ❏ "No" is an appropriate answer (if God deems it so):

    - When we question God's answers, we question His authority. By questioning God, we assume a position of moral authority over

Him—as if He must answer to us, or give an explanation for what He does that satisfies our curiosity or demands.
- We should not think God is only "faithful" when He answers "Yes." God's faithfulness is not dependent on how He answers prayer, but rests upon His countless acts of proven trustworthiness throughout the record of Scripture.

❑ "Wait" is an appropriate answer (if God deems it so):
- We are meant to trust in God's timing, not impose upon Him our own timetable or schedule. Trusting in His schedule is an act of faith; imposing our own schedule is an act of self-will and an attempt to exert control of God's decisions.
- God's timing is superior to ours, since He knows all things past, present, and future, and gauges His responses to us by His omniscience (all-knowingness). Because we lack perfect knowledge, perfect wisdom, and historical perspective, our thoughts about how things should be (or turn out) are inferior to His.

❑ Christians are to have *confidence* that God hears them (1 John 5:14–15). If we pray to God without confidence, then we should not expect to receive anything from Him (James 1:6–8).

❑ Did God hear Jesus' prayers in the Garden (Mat. 26:39, 42)?

- God *did* hear and *did* answer (Heb. 2:7–8). His answer to Jesus' question, "Let this cup pass from Me," was "no." But His answer to Jesus' plea for "Your will [to] be done" was "yes."
- God hears *all* the prayers of His saints (1 Peter 3:12): sometimes He answers "yes," "no," or "wait"—but He *always* answers those who are faithful to Him.
- Paul's own testimony: Rom. 15:30, 2 Cor. 1:11, Col. 4:2–4.

… How does God answer prayer? The short (but accurate) answer is: however He chooses to do so. Since God has proved Himself capable of overcoming every earthly hindrance, every human obstacle, and every circumstantial interference, certainly He still possesses such capabilities. If He wanted to speak to you from the clouds in a thunderous, ground-splitting roar from heaven, He is certainly capable

of doing this. To expect Him to do this—and then to be disappointed when He does not—is not yours to impose upon Him. God is all-powerful and exercises supreme control over all things and every element; He does not need to provide miracles in order to answer prayers. He speaks, and whatever needs to be done is done. How this happens is His decision; it is not yours or mine to dictate.[4]

Your belief in God's ability to perform—really, your decision to let *Him be God—cannot be based upon your pre-scripted plan for your life. In order to draw near to God, you must trust His decisions for you, whether or not they are popular. Once you lay your petition before Him, you give Him the right to decide how that petition will be best answered. You must not place conditions upon your faith in Him, your trust in His judgment, or your confidence in how He answers your prayers. A Christian who prayers to God but does not believe in the* power of prayer *or in the* One to whom prays *is "double-minded" and "unstable in all his ways. As a result, he should not expect to receive* anything *from the Lord, since he manifests not faith in Him, but disbelief (James 1:5–8). You cannot afford to be that person—and you have no* right *to be that person, if indeed God's divine grace has rescued you from your own spiritual ruin!*[5]

- An excellent way to understand and improve our prayer life is to study the book of Psalms.[6] Many of the psalms are in fact prayers to God, and the psalmists knew how to pray effectively. They exhibited great confidence in their prayers (for example, see Psalm 8, 62, and 143). They knew who God was and where they stood with Him. They were not afraid to voice their concerns—even their frustrations (see Psalm 10)—but never at the expense of deep reverence and respect for Him. In fact, "the greatness of the psalmists' prayers comes from their relationship with God. When we view God as they did, we'll begin to pray as they did."[7]

    Obviously, the psalmists believed that God listened to their prayers, otherwise they would not have prayed to Him—and with such sheer

---

[4] Sychtysz, *Seeking the Sacred*, 209–210.

[5] Chad Sychtysz, *Christian Thinking* (Spiritbuilding Publishers, 2016), 218–219.

[6] For this, I recommend my book, *A Study of the Book of Psalms* (Spiritbuilding Publishers, 2020); go to www.booksbychad.com.

[7] Edwin Crozier, *Praying Like the Psalmists: A Study of the Psalms* (Temple Terrace, FL: Florida College Press, 2016), 11.

volume of prayers. They did not believe that God was merely "hearing" their prayers, or logging them as a matter of official record, but that He sought their praises, petitions, and cries for help, and would bring about whatever response He deemed was necessary.

Why do we need to pray? Many people—and many Christians—have asked and continue to ask that question. It is a fair question and deserves a biblical response. There are actually numerous answers, but some dominant ones are listed below. We pray because:

- *God tells us to (Mat. 7:7–8, Col. 4:2, 1 Thess. 5:16–18). If there were no other reasons, this one ought to suffice.*
- *He wants us to (Phil. 4:6).*
- *We need to demonstrate our dependence upon Him (Mat. 6:9–13).*
- *We need to demonstrate humility: He is God, and we are not (1 Peter 5:6–7).*
- *We receive forgiveness only through prayer (1 John 1:9).*
- *We receive wisdom through prayer (Jas. 1:5).*
- *We gain strength through prayer (Eph. 3:14–19).*
- *We gain courage through prayer (Acts 4:24–31).*
- *Prayer is an act of faith, and we are to live by faith (Rom. 1:17).*

How do we know that God hears our prayers? Left to our own finite, earth-bound knowledge, we do not. But—and this is very important—the same Scripture that teaches who God is, what He does, how He responds, and how He saves also teaches that God wants us to pray, hears our prayers, and responds to those prayers. We cannot accept the first premise without also accepting the second, since both are recorded and verified in the same source material. Either we believe all of what God has revealed to us, or we believe none of it.[8]

Please read "In His Time" (page 42) and answer the following:

1.) What are some benefits of having to "wait" on God (and His schedule)?

---

8   Sychtysz, *A Study of the Book of Psalms*, 59–60

2.) "God…is not so concerned with 'time' as He is with *timing*." What do you think this means? How does it apply to prayers and praying?

3.) Why can we not "rush intimacy" or "hurry the sacred"?

4.) How do we put God "to the test" when we insist that He perform according to our own schedule or pre-determined expectations?

- ❑ **Gratitude and prayer:** When we are *genuinely grateful* for what God gives us, does for us, and *is* to us, we will respond in an appropriate manner. Paul wrote to the Philippians, after they had sent a gift (of money and/or provisions) to him: "But I have received everything in full and have an abundance; I am amply supplied, having received from Epaphroditus what you have sent, a fragrant aroma, an acceptable sacrifice, well-pleasing to God. And my God will supply all your needs according to His riches in glory in Christ Jesus. Now to our God and Father be the glory forever and ever. Amen" (Phil. 4:18–20). While the "gift" was *sent* by the Philippians, it ultimately *came* from God's benevolent providence. Paul's attitude was that God is the great Supplier to those who serve Him, and He deserves to be both acknowledged *and* thanked for what He does. If this is true with Paul, it should be just as true with us.

    Gratitude must have a profound effect on a Christian's prayer life. The level of gratitude we have in our hearts affects how we pray, what we pray for, and even whether we pray to God. Our prayers of thanks to God must never be limited to His having fulfilled our wishes and expectations; likewise, we cannot withhold gratitude in every case that He does not perform as we had hoped. Atheists mock Christians—rightly so, at times—when we make a lot of noise for all the good things that God does but are rather quiet about the bad things that He allows to happen (or does not remove). They call this "counting the hits but not the misses." Sadly, this is often true.

It is not uncommon for an announcement concerning a fellow Christian's deliverance from his (or her) ordeal or his physical recovery to be worded as follows: "Brother Frank was released from the hospital today far ahead of his doctor's expectations! So then, God has answered our prayers." This begs the question: if Frank had died, then would this mean that God had not *answered the many prayers offered on his behalf? Or, if Frank had remained in his sickness, then would this mean that God failed to answer such prayers? If He does not answer "yes" to our prayers, do we consider that a so-called "unanswered prayer"? Are we only to praise God for the "yes" answers to our prayers, or should be praise Him for* all *answers?*[9]

Please read "Holding On and Letting Go" (page 44) and answer the following:

1.) What, if anything, does this lesson have to do with prayer?

2.) Have your prayers improved and matured over time—even since a year ago? If yes, how? If not, how can you be drawing near to God by standing still?

3.) Regarding prayers and praying, might there be some long-held or traditional beliefs that you need to let go of—and others that you need to adopt instead? Please explain.

---

[9] Sychtysz, *Christian Thinking*, 216.

The Mechanics of Prayer

- When we pray, should there be (an) appropriate:

    - Intention?
    - Message?
    - Words?
    - Speed?
    - Length?

- Is one's physical posture important?

    In Eph. 3:14, Paul says, "For this reason I bow my knees …"—i.e., he literally assumes a submissive physical posture in presenting this prayer to God on behalf of the Ephesians (and saints everywhere). While we cannot use such passages to impose this posture upon all who pray, there are sufficient references in Scripture to support this as a sign of reverence and voluntary submission to one who is higher in authority:

    - "And a leper came to Him and bowed down before Him, and said, 'Lord, if You are willing, You can make me clean'" (Mat. 8:2)
    - "While He was saying these things to them, a synagogue official [Jairus] came and bowed down before Him, and said, 'My daughter has just died; but come and lay Your hand on her, and she will live'" (Mat. 9:18)
    - "Then the mother of the sons of Zebedee came to Jesus with her sons, bowing down and making a request of Him" (Mat. 20:20)
    - "Seeing Jesus from a distance, he ran up and bowed down before Him…" (Mark 5:6). This passage is particularly remarkable because it is a demon–possessed man who does this. Even the demons know to bow in the presence of God's Son
    - "But after hearing of Him, a woman whose little daughter had an unclean spirit immediately came and fell at His feet" (Mark 7:25).
    - "But when Simon Peter saw that, he fell down at Jesus' feet, saying, 'Go away from me Lord, for I am a sinful man, O Lord!'" (Luke 5:8)

- "Now one of them, when he saw that he had been healed, turned back, glorifying God with a loud voice, and he fell on his face at His feet, giving thanks to Him. And he was a Samaritan" (Luke 17:15–16)
  "Therefore, when Mary came where Jesus was, she saw Him, and fell at His feet, saying to Him, 'Lord, if You had been here, my brother would not have died'" (John 11:32)
- "But what is the divine response to him? 'I have kept for Myself seven thousand men who have not bowed the knee to Baal'" (Rom. 11:4). This passage shows the opposite effect: those who bow in reverence to God must not bow to any other god.
- "For this reason also, God highly exalted Him, and bestowed on Him the name which is above every name, so that at the name of Jesus every knee will bow, of those who are in heaven and on earth and under the earth, and that every tongue will confess that Jesus Christ is Lord, to the glory of God the Father" (Phil. 2:9–11)

The point is clear: it is most appropriate to literally bow one's knees—or one's entire body—in coming before the "throne of grace" (Heb. 4:16). "The bodily attitude during prayer is important, for it reflects the soul's attitude toward God."[10] While bowing or kneeling is not a mandatory requirement, the passages cited illustrate the kind of reverence and respect human beings ought to demonstrate when bringing their petitions—or even their praises (see Rev. 4:9–11)—before the Great King. Such reverence stands in stark contrast to the increasing irreverence and disrespect that characterizes so much of what is called "Christian religion" today.[11]

❏ Some pray to be seen by men (Mat. 6:5–6): this refers to motive, not specific action (contrast with John 11:41–42, for example, where the motive is *appropriate*).

---

10 R. C. H. Lenski, *Commentary on the New Testament: The Interpretation of St. Paul's Epistles to the Galatians, to the Ephesians, and to the Philippians*, vol. 8 (Peabody, MA: Hendrickson Publishers, 1998), 489.

11 Excerpt from Chad Sychtysz, *Galatians and Ephesians Commentary* (Spiritbuilding Publishers, 2024), 82–83.

- Some pray with "many words" (Mat. 6:7): this refers to motive, not specific action (contrast with Psalm 136, for example, where the motive is *appropriate*).

- Prayers are not intended merely to fill a (time) slot in the worship service. For example, while any service may have an "opening" or "closing" prayer, this can easily descend into religious formality, where prayer/praying is simply part of a "worship service" checklist. It is important that church leadership uphold the value and sacredness of prayer to avoid this.

- Prayer is intended to be *meaningful communication* with God; when it ceases to be this, then it becomes something else (i.e., *inferior* or *meaningless* communication).

    - The difference between "meaningful" and "meaningless" is often first manifested in *attitude* (disposition of heart) than in *words* or *content*.

    - However, in pursuit of better prayers, words and content should also improve. Again, deep attention to the psalmists' prayers (in *Psalms*) will elevate the quality and content of our own prayers.

- Prayers—especially public prayers—can become routine, canned, or bland when those offering the prayers seem to be reading from a well-worn script rather than speaking from the heart. For example:

    - **"Dear God"**: while this is not an improper address, it is often a default, uninspired, or worn-out opening. Sometimes Christians simply do not put much thought or creativity in their approach to the throne-room of their Creator. Over time, we ought to have a number of biblical ways to address the Lord.

    - **"Thank you for this day"**: this is often an empty, canned phrase with little depth. It *can* be appropriate, if meant sincerely. Unfortunately, it more often serves as a filler than heartfelt gratitude.

- **"Thank you for the opportunity to assemble together"**: see above.

- **"Thank you for this food"**: often said when praying before a meal. Again, this *can* (and *should*) be appropriate, but only if offered with sincere gratitude rather than simply a filler or go–to phrase. A better or more meaningful expression might be, "Father, we are grateful for this meal that You, through your providence and kindness, have provided for us."

- **"Be with so–and–so …"**: what does this mean? What exactly is being asked? This is perhaps one of the most overused and bland phrases in prayer. We should *be specific* whenever possible, while always deferring to God to have the final say. Many public prayers at church assemblies are filled with "God, please be with so–and–so," without any other information, explanation, or personal advocacy for the one whom we want God to "be" with.

- **"We pray the speaker will have a ready recollection of the things he has studied"**: another well–worn and often–rehearsed phrase. Such phrases are sometimes handed down from parents or previous generations, then repeated by those who have heard them so often. Add to this list, "May the speaker of the hour break unto us the word of life," "May You be merciful to those things which Your pure eyes have seen amiss in our lives," and "Comfort the ailing and afflicted."

- **"Father/Father/Father"** or **"Lord/Lord/Lord"**: this is mindless overuse, often thought to convey reverence but instead are useless, repetitive fillers. In our attempt to be holy, we may think that repeating God's name over and over honors Him, but it may in fact produce the opposite effect (Mat. 6:7).

- **"Guide, guard, and direct us"**: this is an example of one of the traditional phrases that are often spoken without meaning—and often spoken so quickly that no one really has a chance to think about what is being said.

- **"In Jesus' name"**: this is used as a formalized, official, and "biblical" prayer–ender, versus what it is supposed to be—an appeal to Jesus' authority and seeking His intercession. It, too, is often spoken so quickly or unthinkingly that it loses all meaning.

- **"Amen"**: a fitting closing, yet often used formally rather than what it means, which is "yes, yes," "let it be so," or "these words are true." Instead, it is used like a period at the end of a sentence—grammatically correct but lacking in any other meaning.

If *you* have been praying like what has just been described:

1.) What can you do to *improve* your prayers?

2.) Do you *desire* to improve your prayers?

The Lord's Instruction on Prayer

- ❑ The so-called "Lord's Prayer" (Mat. 6:9–13) is really the *disciples'* prayer: it was given *by* the Lord but is intended *for* His disciples. It is not meant to be a formalized, word-for-word prayer that is rehearsed repeatedly and often without thought (as is often done today in some denominational churches). Rather, it is meant only to be a *model* or *basic template* of how one is to pray to God ("Pray, then, *in this way* …"—Mat. 6:9):

    - **"Our Father"**: an appropriate address of God (as the Giver of life). God is very rarely ever addressed as "Father" in the Old Testament. But Jesus' sermon on the mount (which is the context for this present teaching) anticipates a *new covenant relationship* with God through Christ. This involves a "new" way of approaching God—no longer as a mere authority figure but also as One with paternal concern for His children "in Christ."

- **"who is in heaven"**: a separation between our nature and God's (Eccles. 5:2–3). In prayer, we are meant to elevate our thoughts to where God is, and never try to bring His majesty down to where we are.[12] Since God is in heaven (and we are not), we are to defer to His authority, wisdom, discernment, and justice rather than insist upon our own.

- **"Hallowed is Your name"**: God is sacred, incomparable, and the source of holiness; He deserves to be honored and revered above all other beings. "Hallowed" is an archaic expression of "holy," adopted from the KJV Bible (1611). God is holy regardless of whether we acknowledge Him as such, so the prayer is not "God, please be holy"—because He is *intrinsically* holy—but "God, You are holy *to me*—Your name is holy to *my heart*." (Compare 1 Peter 3:15: "sanctify Christ as Lord in your hearts.")

- **"Your kingdom come"**: this anticipated what Jesus preached (Mark 1:15) but since has been fulfilled (Acts 8:12, 28:31, Rev. 12:10, etc.). The "kingdom," from Acts 2 forward, is nearly always viewed as a yet-to-be-inherited promise, not a present reality. Those who are "in Christ" are presently in His church—a present reality—but we have yet to experience the eternal kingdom (see Acts 14:22, 2 Tim. 4:18, Heb. 11:16, 2 Peter 1:10–11, etc.). Yet we can now say, "Your kingdom *has* come," "May Your kingdom be preached," "May the power and authority of Your kingdom through Christ bring about Your will in every realm," etc.

- **"Your will be done …"**: we are to submit to Christ's will, whether in the world or our personal lives. Because Jesus now rules as King (Acts 2:33), His will is "done" through the obedience of those who belong to Him (Rom. 6:12–13).

---

12 "[This] also emphasizes another aspect of our relationship with Him: not only father and child, but creator and creature. There is balance here: we address God intimately as Father while recognizing His infinite greatness in heaven" (Nathan Ward, *Our Eyes Are on You: A Biblical Study of Prayer* [Tampa, FL: DeWard Publishing Co., Ltd., 2023], 199).

We should never pray, "Your will be done," without also pledging allegiance and obedience to that will.

- **"… on earth as it is in heaven"**: in the Greek text of this passage, this phrase applies to all three of the preceding phrases ("hallowed is Your name," "Your kingdom come," and "Your will be done").[13] The prayer, then, supports God's work in the spiritual realm as well as the physical realm. No one should be praying these things unless they see themselves as active participants in *carrying out* that work in whatever way God intends for them (see Eph. 2:10)

- **"Give us this day …"**: dependence upon God for all necessary provisions is appropriate, spiritually healthy, and an act of humility. All that is good in our lives can be traced back to Him; "Every good thing given and every perfect gift is from above, coming down from the Father of lights" (James 1:17).

- **"And forgive us our debts …"**: forgiveness is at the core of the gospel message (Luke 24:46–47). It is useless to seek God's forgiveness if we refuse to have a forgiving heart toward those who sin against us (Mat. 18:21–35).[14] This is a simple concept yet remains (for many Christians) one of the most difficult and often resisted instructions from the Lord (see also Eph. 4:32 and Col. 3:12–14).

- **"And do not lead us into temptation …"**: in other words, believe that God will (and always does) provide a "way of escape" from whatever tempts you (1 Cor. 10:13). He is not tempted *with* sin and does not tempt us *to* sin (James 1:13). However, not all "temptation" involves being seduced to do what is wrong; some temptations (or "trials"—James 1:2–4) are meant to test whether we will do what is *right*. Such was the case of Jesus being "led up by the Spirit into the wilderness to be tempted by the devil" (Mat. 4:1). In such

---

13   Ward, *Our Eyes Are on You*, 199.

14   For a full study on "forgiveness," I recommend my book, *The Gospel of Forgiveness* (Spiritbuilding Publishers, 2021); go to www.spiritbuilding.com/chad.

cases, God is not inciting us to fail but just the opposite: to turn to Him for deliverance—just as Jesus did.

In this one model prayer, our relationship with God is depicted in several different ways:

Expression:	Relationship:
Our Father	father and child
Hallowed by Your name	God and worshiper
Your kingdom come	king and subject
Your will be done	master and servant
Give us this day…	benefactor and suppliant
Forgive us our debts…	creditor and debtor
Lead us not into temptation	guide and pilgrim
Deliver us…	redeemer and redeemed[15]

❑ Jesus also taught His disciples to be asking, seeking, and knocking through prayer (Mat. 7:7–11, 21:22, and Mark 11:24):

- What does it mean (or imply) to "ask" God for something?

  – Should you expect to receive if you do not ask (see James 4:2b)?

  – How should you receive His answer?

- What does it mean to "seek" in the way Jesus describes?

  – Is what you seek according to His will (see James 4:3, 1 John 5:14)?

  – What will you do once He reveals what you had sought?

- What does it mean to "knock" in the way Jesus describes?

---

15 Chart from Ward, *Our Eyes Are on You*, 205.

- What do you hope to find on the other side of the "door"?

- What will you do if He opens it—or if He keeps it closed? Do you honor Jesus' decision in either case (Rev. 3:7)?

Someone asks, "Why would Christ lead anyone to a closed door?" We might answer rhetorically: Why did God give to Abraham a son of promise (Isaac) only to ask him to sacrifice that son as a burnt offering? Why did God lead Israel out of Egypt only to dead-end their journey at the shore of the Red Sea? Why did Christ's disciples train for three years, only to watch their Teacher's life be snuffed out in a gruesome and seemingly untimely death? In all of these examples, God led people to a closed door. God brought Abraham, Israel, and Christ's disciples to a door that could not be opened by anyone but Him. The lesson, then, was to prove God's supernatural ability to open doors that no one else could open. Thus, God opened the door to Abraham's future by sparing his son Isaac through a vicarious sacrifice (of a ram). God opened the door to Israel's future by parting the Red Sea. And God opened the door to the disciples' ministries by shattering the bonds of death through His Son's resurrection.

If God can open these doors, can He not open doors for you? "But not all doors are meant to be opened," someone says, and this is true. Christ opens doors that He wants opened but closes doors that He wants closed. You've heard it said that every time one door closes, another opens: this seems to be generally the case. It might be even more accurate to say… that every time Christ closes a door, **many others may be opened.** *We should not limit the One who possesses all the resources of heaven and earth to having only a few doors to work with!*[16]

---

16 Sychtysz, *Seeking the Sacred,* 221.

What to Pray For

- **Prayer is objective or goal-oriented in nature:** there is always a *reason* for it to be done. No Christian should ever offer a useless, mindless, or hopeless prayer. God is always purposeful in whatever He does. He sends His word out into the world, and it always accomplishes His will (Isa. 55:10–11). He sends preachers out into the world, and they proclaim His eternal purpose (Rom. 10:14–15, Phil. 1:15–18). He sent His Son into the world, and He accomplished everything God wanted Him to do (John 17:3–4). The point is: when we exercise God's gifts (such as prayer), we should never think that they will not bring about good. At the same time, we should never use those gifts in ways for which they were never intended. For example:

  - We should never pray for a miracle because there is no *reason* to expect one.
  - We should never pray for God to forgive those who impenitently rebel against Him, or who are not "in Christ," because there is no *reason* He will do this (1 John 5:16).
  - We should never pray for God to remove all problems, struggles, bad experiences, enemies, or our "cross" (Mat. 16:24), because there is no *reason* for such requests.

- We tend to pray for personal comfort, personal safety, and good health. Naturally, we do not want to suffer if we can avoid it—this is a human default response. On the other hand:

  - This often assumes that the absence of comfort, safety, and health are always disadvantageous (but this is not true). All spiritual growth occurs *outside* of our comfort zone, not within it. By habitually praying for God to protect our comfort zone (or status quo), we are inadvertently praying to remain unchanged, untransformed, and complacent with our present spiritual condition.
  - This assumes, when we pray for the health (or healing) of others, it is always in their best interest to be healthy (or healed)—but this may not be true. God may use sickness for His glory (John

9:1–3, 11:4), or even for discipline of the impenitent (1 Cor. 11:29–30, Rev. 2:22). There is nothing wrong with asking for God's healing; there *is* something wrong with expecting Him to heal simply because we asked.
- We should be careful not to put comfort, safety, and health ahead of discipleship to Christ. We can *want* these things—and pray for them—but we must not allow the pursuit of them to interfere with seeking God's will above our own.

❑ A Christian might pray to *avoid* cross–bearing rather than for strength to *carry* his cross. Or he may pray to have problems *removed* rather than seeking God's grace to overcome *despite* them. Or he may pray for others to do the work that he is fully capable of doing himself. In each case, *self–protection* is put ahead of *submissive discipleship.* Such is a misuse of prayer: even though prayers are being asked, they are not entirely seeking God's interests ahead of one's own (Mat. 16:23, 1 John 5:14–15)

❑ We tend to want to "jump ship" because of **fear** rather than having **faith** to ride out the storm (and to leave the ship only when *God* says to do so—see Acts 27:30–31)

Please read "Praying for One Another" (page 46) and answer the following:

1.) Is there any harm in praying only (or predominantly) for ourselves and not for others? What does this say about us? About our concern for fellow believers?

2.) What benefits do we personally gain by praying for others? Are we *expected* to pray for others, or is it simply a nice gesture when we do?

3.) Does the content of our prayers reveal our true disposition toward our "brother" in Christ (1 John 2:7–10)? What does Christ expect this disposition to be (John 13:34–35)?

Christians can stray from the truth: they can habitually spurn Christ's gospel, the terms of our salvation. Such wandering or straying endangers one's spiritual well-being. Sometimes a person needs help getting out of that danger and back to where he should be. Those who are spiritual, wise, and well-grounded in the faith can offer this help in the form of encouragement, persuasion, and prayerful entreaty (James 5:19–20; Gal. 6:1–2). Such a person can turn the wayward or wandering Christian back to his original commitment to the Lord and help to rekindle his dwindling faith. James says, "Let him [the one who offers this help—MY WORDS] know…"—i.e., it is a tremendous and noble deed to rescue someone from his own spiritual peril (Jude 1:22–23).

Those who engage in this work ought to be aware of how important it is. It is incorrect to say that the one who helped to turn him back is also fully responsible for that person's restoration; on the other hand, it is true that he played a vital part in this and should be commended for his efforts. Ultimately, however, each person is responsible for his own soul's disposition before God. The sinner who is turned "from the error of his way" will be saved from (spiritual) death and the forgiveness he receives from the Lord will "cover a multitude of [his own] sins." This means it is not important how many sins are "covered," only that they are covered through the grace of God (1 Peter 4:8). No matter how capable or willing to help a person may be, he cannot override the wayward Christian's moral responsibility to God for his own soul. "Cover" here does not mean "hide" or "conceal," but to take care of in an appropriate manner, as when God "covers" our sins through an appeal to Christ's blood (Rom. 4:7, 1 John 1:7).[17]

- ❏ "The effective prayer of a righteous man can accomplish much" (James 5:16).

    - What does this mean? What does this *not* mean?

    - What does this *require* of us if we want our own prayers to be "effective"?

The extent of what God can accomplish through the righteous man is illustrated

---

[17] Excerpt from Chad Sychtysz, *Titus and James Commentary* (Spiritbuilding Publishers, 2024), 110–111.

by the case of Elijah—a mortal human being just like us—whose prayerful entreaty to God both caused and then ended a three-and-a-half-year drought in Israel (James 5:17–18; see 1 Kings 17:1 and 18:1). This does not mean God will respond in this same way (or with any miraculous demonstration) because of our prayers, but simply highlights the fact that prayer is not an ineffective measure, when accompanied by faith. Just as God answered Elijah's prayer, so He will answer the faithful Christian's prayer. Whether He does so is certain; how He does so is left up to Him. Contrast this with the one who prays but does not believe and is thus "double-minded"; that person should not expect to receive anything from God (James 1:5–8). God will act on behalf of the prayers of His righteous people; He has no reason to act for those who will not believe in His power.[18]

General Topics of Prayer

- ❑ In general, we can pray:

    - Not only for friends and loved ones but also our enemies (Mat. 5:44).
    - For all men, especially those in authority (1 Tim. 2:1–3).
    - For our nation, especially when it is heading for disaster (2 Chron. 7:14).
    - That workers might reach the lost (Mat. 9:38, Luke 10:2).
    - For spiritual completion (2 Cor. 13:9).
    - For enlightenment (Eph. 1:18, Col. 1:9–10).
    - For divine strength (Eph. 3:14–16).
    - For help "beyond all that we ask or think" (Eph. 3:20).
    - For real knowledge and discernment (Phil. 1:9).
    - When suffering or physically ill (James 5:13–15).
    - For one another (during confession of sins) (James 5:16).
    - For good health (3 John 2).
    - For a better, healthier marriage (1 Cor. 7:5).

- ❑ The four "alls" of prayer (Eph. 6:18):

    - **All** kinds (petition, appeal for help, and praise).
    - **All** times (in times of ease and prosperity as well as times of trouble and deprivation).

---

18   *Ibid.*, 110.

- **All** perseverance (Luke 11:5–10, 18:1–8).
- Petition for **all** the saints (not just the ones you know by name or are friends with).

Please read "Giving Thanks" (page 48) and answer the following:

1.) Given the examples in Scripture, is it appropriate to give thanks before a meal?

2.) What good can come from "giving thanks" beyond simply thanking God for the meal?

3.) When we give thanks in public, how should this be conducted—and why?

- ❏ Consider Jesus' own prayer life:
    - While being baptized, He was praying (Luke 3:21).
    - He "would often slip away to the wilderness and pray" (Luke 5:16).
    - At times, He sent everyone away and went to pray by Himself throughout the night (Mat. 14:23, Luke 6:12).
    - In the early morning while it was still dark, He would leave the house and go to a secluded place to pray (Mark 1:35).
    - He spent entire night in prayer before appointing the twelve disciples (Luke 6:12–19).
    - His reason for ascending the mountain (of transfiguration) in Caesarea Philippi was to pray with Peter, James, and John (Luke 9:28–29).
    - Jesus prayed for Peter; "and you, once you have turned again, strengthen your brothers" (Luke 22:32).
- ❏ What does this information tell us about:
    - The importance of prayer in Jesus' life?
    - The occasional need for solitude and privacy in prayer?

- Praying instead of sleeping (in some cases)?
- Praying before making any major decision(s)?

☐ Please read Jesus' prayer in John 17:1–26:

- Is this a prayer we can *pray*, or is it a prayer we can *learn* from?

- Will one be glorified *before* suffering or *after* it (see Rom. 8:16–17)?

- Why did Jesus defer to God as the Source of eternal life (see 1 John 5:11, 20)?

- What was Jesus' mission? (What is yours?)

- Did Jesus just *talk* about God's will or did He in fact *fulfill* it?

- Did Jesus pray only for Himself?

- Did Jesus ask that His disciples be removed from all danger or discomfort?

- "Sanctify them in the truth; Your word is truth" (17:17)—what does this mean?

- Why did Jesus pray for unity? Does unnecessary division among Christians honor His prayer?

- What will be the outcome of those who are "one" with God?

- Did Jesus provide a sufficient example of His love for His disciples to follow?

The God to whom we pray is a God who wants us to be united to Him. Even as there is pure unity within God, He desires unity within the body of His people leading to oneness between the body and the Head. He cares so much about this, in fact, that it was a chief concern in His final prayer, a deeply personal prayer He shares with the apostles—and with anyone who reads John's gospel.[19]

- ❑ We are told to pray *in* the Spirit (but never *to* Him) (Eph. 6:18, Jude 1:20).

    - What does this mean?

    - What does this *not* mean?

- ❑ Please read Rom. 8:26–27.

    - What does this passage mean?

    - What does it *not* mean?

- ❑ The "full armor of God" is never "full" or complete without prayer (Eph. 6:10–18).

    It would be well for the soldier who goes forth to battle to pray ... for victory; or to pray that he may be prepared for death, should he fall. But soldiers do not often feel the necessity of this. To the Christian soldier, however, it is indispensable. Prayer crowns all lawful efforts with success, and gives a victory when nothing else would. No matter how complete the armour [sic]; no matter how skilled we maybe in the science of war; no matter how courageous we may be, we may be certain that without prayer we shall be defeated. God alone can give the victory; and when the Christian soldier goes forth armed completely for the spiritual conflict, if he looks to God by prayer, he may be sure of a triumph. This prayer is not to be intermitted. It is to be always. In every temptation and spiritual conflict we are to pray.[20]

---

19 Ward, *Our Eyes Are on You*, 206.
20 Albert Barnes, *Barnes' Notes*, electronic edition (database © 2014 by WORDsearch

- ❑ The relationship between prayer and fasting (Mat. 6:16–18, 17:21, Acts 13:3, and 14:23): one is commanded, the other is not; *both* are instrumental in seeking intimacy with God.

    - Fasting (in Scripture): the intentional deprivation of food (and other comforts) for the purpose of drawing near to God or seeking divine favor (Lev. 16:29–30).

    - What fasting means to God: Isa. 58:3–7.

    - Prayer is an integral part of fasting but fasting is not required to pray.

- ❑ Prayers in song (or prayers put to music): such songs are specifically addressed to God to petition for certain things, appeal for His help, or offer praise to His name.

    - What do these songs (below) communicate?

    - What is the attitude or disposition of the one who "speaks" in the song?

    - Should anyone be "praying" these songs if he does not honor what they say?

    - If anyone *does* honor them, how should this be evident?

Corp.), on Eph. 6:18.

"How Great Thou Art"	"O Jesus I Have Promised"
"Great Is Thy Faithfulness" (Lam. 3:23–24)	"I Am Thine, O Lord"
"I Stand in Awe"	"Take My Life, and Let It Be"
"As the Deer" (Psalm 42:1–2)	"In His Time"
"Come Thou Almighty King"	"Listen to Our Hearts"
"Glorify Thy Name" (Psalm 86:12)	"Jesus, Let Us Come to Know You"
"Be Exalted O God" (Psalm 57:11)	"Take My Hand, Precious Lord"
"Jesus, the Very Thought of Thee"	"Thy Word" (Psalm 119:105)
"Just a Closer Walk with Thee"	"I Bring My Sins to Thee"
"Be Thou My Vision"	"My Savior Dear, I Love Thee"

Final Thoughts

- ❏ Christians are to be "devoted to prayer" (Rom. 12:12, Col. 4:2, 1 Thess. 5:17)

    - What does this mean?

    - What does this *not* mean?

- ❏ Prayer is often spoken of as an "exercise." Why is this depiction so appropriate?

- ❏ In prayer, we give to God what we are unable to bear on our own, and we receive from Him what we are unable to obtain on our own. Do you agree with this?

- ❏ Has this class given you a deeper awareness and understanding of prayer?

- ❏ Have you experienced positive changes in your "extra" prayers for the sake of this class?

Intimacy with God

For someone to be close to you, you must get close to that person. Likewise, if you wish God to "draw near" to you, you must "draw near" to Him (James 4:8). God desires fellowship with your soul above all else. There is much to be gained in such intimacy (Eph. 3:16–19) and it is all yours for the asking. But you cannot leap into an "intimate relationship" with God (or anyone else) without understanding what intimacy is in the first place.

"Intimacy" is that which is private and personal. It can take place on various levels: physical, emotional, intellectual, and spiritual. Intimacy is a deliberate choice made by two people; it is never accidental, assumed, or automatic. Intimacy ought to be experienced in marriage, but it is not necessary to be married (or even related, or even of the opposite sex) to have an intimate relationship with someone. For example, "kindred spirits" are those who enjoy spiritually intimate friendships (Phil. 2:19–20). Married couples may perceive "intimacy" on several different levels, and it can be equally rewarding for both parties.

Intimacy cannot exist without proper communication. Intimacy is not just "talking" or "sex," though intimacy can involve both (and more). Communication occurs when two people are sending, receiving, *and* replying to various messages between them. Both people must participate for this to happen. Intimate communication requires a sharing of oneself *with* another, thus a giving of oneself *to* another. This requires a revealing of oneself (a.k.a. self–disclosure), which makes it difficult for those who do not know (yet) how to do this, have had poor role models, or are afraid to reveal themselves with such depth (for whatever reason). However, none of these difficulties are insurmountable. Self–disclosure can create a certain sense of vulnerability in the one doing the revealing. If he (or she) trusts the one to whom he is disclosing himself, he will not be threatened by this; if he does not, then he will likely not reveal much at all. One who enjoys an intimate relationship with God usually can communicate intimately with people, since he has no secret sins to hide; he practices self–disclosure already; he trusts God to vindicate him (1 Cor. 4:3–5); he does not live by fear (of being exposed or exploited).

Those who have been Christians for many years ought to have already developed an intimate relationship with God. Those who are stuck on elementary things (Heb. 5:12) or are still immature in their thinking (1 Cor. 3:1–3) will not have this intimacy—but this can all change. Self-disclosure can be a difficult and uncomfortable experience at first; over time, however, it can be liberating and rewarding. Intimacy cannot be forced or demanded; you must voluntarily consent to it—and so must God. One's "interior life" (the core of which is your *soul*) is a very private and intense realm; in prayer, you reveal this realm to God. In essence, you invite God into fellowship with your soul. While He already knows your thoughts and spirit (Heb. 4:12–13), when you disclose yourself to Him, you are saying, "I trust You." Specifically, you trust that He will not betray your confidences; He will not judge you unfairly or unnecessarily; He will expose your faults only to correct and refine you; He will be kind to you and concerned for you with a fatherly concern. The same Spirit by which you pray (Rom. 8:26) also searches the Mind of God (1 Cor. 2:10), bringing you a deeper understanding of God in return. As you pray to Him privately, so you also pray with the most private *part* of you (consider in "inner room" in Mat. 6:6 as having a double meaning, as the sanctuary of your soul). In prayer, you give to God what you cannot bear, and receive from Him what you cannot acquire otherwise.

Intimacy with people is not guaranteed but it *must* be present in one's relationship with God. Those who are afraid of intimacy must confess that they are afraid of God (or of what He is asking of them), for this is what such resistance implies. It makes no sense why a child of God would deliberately refuse to draw closer to Him. But those who pursue an intimate relationship with Him are grateful for the privilege and find great joy in exploring the mind of God through prayer and the study of His word.

Having a Thirst for God

Every good salesman knows that you cannot sell a product until you create a need. This applies in the spiritual context as well: people will not drink of God's "living water" unless they realize their desperate thirst for it in the first place. Our "thirst" for God is not something we personally will into existence but is something we discover and then nurture over time. This thirst has always existed, whether we have recognized it for what it is. However, we can *enhance* this thirst by a better understanding of the needs of our human spirit and how God fulfills them.*

God is the Source of completion for all our soul's needs. In Jer. 2:13, God condemned Judah for deserting Him and depending instead on "broken cisterns"—a metaphorical reference to their idols. (A cistern was usually a limestone– and plaster–lined underground pit for water storage.) God provides "living water" leading to eternal life; in sharp contrast, a man–made cistern is unable to provide anything nourishing to the soul. Yet people today also abandon God's "living water" for wells they have dug themselves. This undoubtedly implies that we are all "thirsty" for something more than our everyday existence can quench.

"Thirst" implies incompletion. Attempting to quench the soul's thirst by one's own power is to reject God's power. Self–sufficiency is not a matter of faith but of pride; it is not only impossible to maintain but is condemned by God. People who abandon God and what He offers remain thirsty but try to relieve their thirst in hopeless ways. Jesus said that, to satisfy our spiritual thirst, we must come to Him for "living water" (i.e., the life–giving Holy Spirit—John 7:37–39). Some people know of no other source of water than man–made wells (John 4:10–15) and are thus ignorant of this "living water." Even some Christians who claim to be "living in God" may not be *drinking from His Spirit*. As a result, they are literally dying of spiritual thirst.

We all have longings and desires. But some longings are more important than others. The human soul longs for creature comforts (casual longings); fulfilling relationships with people (critical longings); a relationship with a Higher Being (crucial longings). This last "longing" does *not* necessarily mean that everyone craves God Himself, but that it is natural for people to seek validation for their existence by supra–human authority. At the same time, a longing for God cannot be reduced to a church membership or mere Christian status, but refers to a meaningful, intimate *communion* with God. While many people spend their lives working on the first two "longings," this latter one is paramount.

Many people try to quench the soul's longing for God with physical comforts, relationships with others, narcotics, addictions, religious piety, and even self–sacrifice (martyrdom) in one form or another. Such people are trying to duplicate the *experience* of intimacy with God through something (or someone) much less fulfilling than Him. In doing so, they are digging their own wells, hoping to quench their thirst and find completion or happiness through whatever they find enjoyable. Others may come to Christ not to drink of His Spirit but to find relief for their pain. But God does not promise relief from physical suffering; He promises the fulfillment of one's spiritual life. "Living water" is not intended to remove physical pain, heartache, loneliness, emptiness, or rejection.

Christ does not want us to ignore our soul's "thirst" but to be painfully aware of it. First, He wants us to know that for which we *are* thirsty. What we *describe* as mere bad habits (e.g., outbursts of anger, excessive materialism, obsession with social media, etc.) are in fact failed attempts at digging our own wells—i.e., reacting to our "thirst" for God in a very worldly manner. Second, He wants us to experience the humility of coming to *Him* to relieve our thirst rather than proudly trying to quench it on our own. The first step in humility is knowing who it is that needs to change: Christ, others, or us. (It will never be Christ and is probably not "others.") We will not welcome Christ's solution if we think the problem belongs to someone else (Psalm 139:23–24). We must clean the *inside* (our heart) first before the outside (actions) has any meaning (Mat. 23:26). This cleansing (of one's conscience) begins with baptism (1 Peter 3:21) but continues with daily presentations before the "throne of grace" (Heb. 4:14–16). Third, Christ wants us to feel the *pain* of an aching thirst. He wants us parched, gasping, and begging for "living water" (His Spirit) rather than having a passive, casual desire for Him. He wants us to realize the inadequacy of this world—and our own power—in taking care of our thirst.

Christians who refuse to come to Christ to satisfy their thirst will not become better saints. Instead, they will become smug, overconfident, and often delusional people. Such people practice a religion of self–sufficiency, not humble dependence upon God's Spirit. They are not drinking from Christ's "living water" but from their own self-dug well. Christ, however, invites us to recognize our thirst and then "come" to Him for what will satisfy it. His inexhaustible supply of "living water" is beyond our ability to duplicate. Through Him we have full access to this "water" (Rev. 22:1, 17). Our spiritual longings will not be satisfied by *any other source* but God. For this reason, we are strongly encouraged to obey Christ's invitation to "Come!"

* Some information in this article is based upon *Inside Out* by Dr. Larry Crabb (Multnomah, 1988), 83ff.

We Have an Advocate

Having a capable lawyer in a court of law can give you great confidence when you stand before the judge. Even if *you* have never had to stand before a judge, *every person* will someday stand before the judgment seat of Christ (2 Cor. 5:10). Many will have no one to intercede or speak for them: those who (by choice) do not know God and those who (having known Him) lived in disobedience to Him. However, Christ will speak on behalf of those who have been faithful to Him (1 John 2:1–2): He will be their righteous "Advocate."

An "advocate" (in classical usage) is one called alongside a defendant to speak for him in a court of law. He is also known as a patron, intercessor, or counselor. The Old Testament is filled with those who served as advocates for others (often for Israel): Noah, Abraham, Job, Moses, Samuel, Daniel, and the prophets in general. Sometimes their intercession was successful (as in Exod. 32:11–14). At other times, however, it was not: Abraham's intercession could not save Sodom (Gen. 18:23–33); Jeremiah could not pray for Judah (Jer. 7:16); and Ezekiel was told that no advocacy could spare Jerusalem (Ezek. 14:13–14). Likewise, Christians are told not to intercede for one who will not repent of his sins (1 John 5:16).

Jesus is the consummate Advocate for those who are unable to defend (or speak for) themselves. During His ministry, He spoke for children (Mat. 18:1–11), vindicated a man born blind (John 9:35–39), rose to Mary's defense (John 12:7), and spoke to the Father on behalf of His disciples (John 17:12). Jesus' advocacy is always successful; no one is disappointed who trusts in Him (John 10:27–30). The Greek word translated "Advocate" (in 1 John 2:1) is translated elsewhere as "Comforter" or "Helper" (John 14:16, etc.). There is no conflict in regarding both the Holy Spirit *and* Jesus as Advocates, for they both intercede for us in special ways. The Holy Spirit carries our prayers and requests to heaven (Rom. 8:26), while Jesus intercedes for us at the right hand of God (8:34). Jesus' ascension to God is the *reason* we have the Spirit's intercession (John 16:7). The Father loves whomever Jesus loves and gives His Spirit to whomever Jesus endorses (16:26–27).

We ought not to think of Christ's advocacy as merely legal representation. Lawyers usually placate the judge and jury with smooth words, shrewd legal maneuvers, and emotional manipulations. Jesus speaks only with wisdom and grace; He does not manipulate anything or anyone. Whatever He says is true, binding, and unbiased. As our Advocate, He is our High Priest—"Jesus Christ the *righteous*" (1 John 2:1, emphasis added). He is righteous by His own intrinsic worthiness; therefore, His words are always heard, and the Father always agrees with them. In acquitting us, He removes all our guilt and shame, and thus comforts and consoles us. But He is also the *offering* ("propitiation") that a High Priest offers (1 John 2:2). This sacrifice of appeasement (His body and blood) bears and absorbs the penalty of our offenses. In so doing, He satisfies the wrath of God toward us, fulfilling perfect justice in Himself (Rom. 5:9). People are fallible; our High Priest is not (Heb. 7:23–28).

Jesus will not intercede for just anyone, however. For Christ to be his Advocate, a person must have a right relationship with Him. Otherwise, he is nothing but a stranger to the Lord, and He will not speak for strangers (Mat. 7:21–23). Such a person will face the wrath of God full strength, without any defense or recourse. Likewise, if one fails to "confess" Christ (i.e., in his lifestyle, not merely through verbal confession), then He will not confess him before the Father—He will not speak as his Advocate (Mat. 10:32–33). Christ also will not advocate for those who fail to forgive others (Mat. 6:14–15, 18:21–35), or for those who condemn their own brethren, especially over matters of opinion and not law (Rom. 14:10–12, James 4:11–12).

Christ will never condemn the innocent. But one is only *made* innocent through his obedience to the gospel of Christ, having been cleansed by Christ's blood (Heb. 9:22). Our responsibility is to come to Him in faith; "whoever believes in Him will not be disappointed" (Rom. 10:11). Your turn to stand before the Judge is coming; you would be wise to *prepare yourself* for that time. The only way to be so prepared is to seek the advocacy of Jesus Christ as He has instructed you.

In His Time

"Good things come to those who wait." While this may imply some general truths, it is *not* true that waiting *by itself* brings about "good things"; that patience automatically makes one righteous; or that patience equates to salvation. Those who will not depend upon God will not see salvation, no matter how patient they may claim to be. God "causes all things to work together for good" only to those who love Him and are called by Him (Rom. 8:28). A "good" future depends upon His having *called* us and our having *loved* Him. "In hope we have been saved," and therefore we eagerly wait upon God to act in His time (Rom. 8:24–25).

"Waiting" is a very human experience since God does not regard time in the same way we do. He is an eternal Divine Being who lives in an ever-present existence. He operates by *sequences* (the order of things, e.g., Rom. 1:16, Heb. 1:1–2) and *conditions* (the fulfillment of certain requirements, e.g., Gen. 15:16, Rom. 5:6). He is not so concerned with "time" as He is with *timing*. This fact directly affects how He responds to our prayers. Time does not change His will or who He is (Heb. 13:8); but He may delay, defer, and show restraint in whatever manner serves our best interests. Sometimes God makes us wait on purpose to see if we will truly trust Him. There are numerous stories in the Bible of those who have had to wait days, months, years, and decades for God: Jonah (3 days in the deep); Joshua (7 days to destroy Jericho); Israel (40 days for Moses); Joseph (13 years in prison); Abraham (25 years for Isaac); Israel (40 years in the wilderness); etc. To "wait" in Scripture often means "to hope in" or "look expectantly toward." This is a matter of faith (Heb. 11:1–2) since we must "hope" for what we cannot see while still believing that it does exist.

There are good lessons to learn from waiting (Psalm 25:4–5). We learn discipleship through waiting on the Master for His leadership and timing. Just as Jesus tarried over responding to Lazarus' sickness, so He may tarry concerning us—perhaps to be glorified *through* us (John 11:6). God is so powerful that He can accomplish His will *without* hurrying or responding right away. Also, since we have seen "the goodness of the Lord" toward others (Psalm 27:11–14), we have every reason to believe He will bring about goodness for us. People let us down; we often let *ourselves* down; but God never truly disappoints anyone (Rom. 10:11–13). The more we learn to wait upon and trust in Him, the more our relationship with Him deepens. Christ's promise toward us is faithful (2 Tim. 2:11–13); for this reason, we can have great confidence in His priestly intercession (Heb. 7:25). Since His intercession is real, our hope in Him is worthwhile and intensifying.

Lasting friendships take time to build. Once they are established, they may last for years, decades, or even a lifetime. Likewise, our "friendship" with Christ takes time to blossom and mature, and He is patient to wait for *us*. One cannot rush intimacy or hurry the sacred, yet a deep relationship with Christ will endure beyond our own physical existence. "For this reason," we ought to be willing to persevere in our faith in Him, even to suffer loss for Him (2 Tim. 1:12). On the other hand, it is a contradiction to teach that we should "wait on God" while insisting that He act as soon as we petition Him. One is a "need," the other is a "want"; we are to exercise discernment between the two. Furthermore, we often take years to create our own problems, and it is unfair—and offensive—to expect God to literally "fix" everything overnight. We are not to "put the Lord…to the test" (Mat. 4:7), and we most certainly *do* "test" Him when we insist that He perform a miracle before we will believe in Him.

God's power is "perfected in [human] weakness" (2 Cor. 12:9). In other words, God *could* work more quickly if He wanted to, but because He is omniscient and omnipotent, He does not *have* to. This also means He is not any less "God" when He does not meet our expectations of the speed of His progress. The attitude we should have is expressed in Psalm 62:1–2: "My soul waits in silence for God only; from Him is my salvation. He only is my rock and my salvation, my stronghold; I shall not be greatly shaken." Good things *do* come to those who wait, but only to those who wait upon God in obedient faith. We will not have to wait forever, however; in due time, He will act, and we shall see Him.

Holding On and Letting Go

In many cases, some of what we call "personal beliefs" in fact came from someone else. At one point, we grabbed a hold of this idea and made it our own. Over time, however, our sense of *pride* or how this idea contributes to our *personal identity* makes it difficult to let go of it. We are not supposed to become slaves of men (1 Cor. 7:23) *or* of any person's belief that contradicts God's word. Even so, sometimes we choose to be enslaved by another person's way of thinking to the extent that it imprisons our own. What began as "This is what I choose to believe" may over time be elevated to "I cannot possibly think otherwise." Yet just as we once *chose* an idea, so we can *un–*choose it. Whatever did not come from God must be deemed changeable and expendable. Whatever belongs to men will not survive for long; only that which comes from God Himself is of lasting value (Mat. 15:13, 1 John 2:16–17).

If you are a Christian, then you have been purchased by God with the blood of Christ. "You are not your own" (1 Cor. 6:19–20) means that you no longer have *controlling interest* over yourself, your thoughts, or your behavior. Whatever you do must be done for Christ, not for yourself. The Lord does allow you to have private opinions and convictions, but these must not interfere with or contradict His will for you. His will takes precedence over yours: His wisdom is better than yours; His thoughts are higher and superior to your own; He must be "Lord" to you. Thus, no matter how dearly you have come to believe one thing or another, if Christ says that it must be otherwise, then it *must be otherwise.* Even if you have maintained a certain position on something for many years, Christ's "position" must supersede your own. We may struggle with this—not because we are trying to be difficult, but because it goes against our pride, emotions, and/or personal identity. Yet if our identity is "in Christ," then there really is no value in pursuing an identity separate from this. Belonging to Christ must be made more important than belonging to an opposing point–of–view. Conforming to the heavenly standard and being transformed into His image must be made more important to us than maintaining our opinions.

We are told to leave elementary thinking behind and press on to maturity (Heb. 6:1). To do the one (press on to maturity) requires that we first let go of the other (elementary thinking). We cannot cling to both at the same time; we cannot move *forward* and *stand still* all at once. Concepts like "growth," "maturity," and "transformation" always require this: letting go of one thing to hold onto the other. Sometimes Christians will say, "I want to become more spiritual," but they will not always be willing to release their grip on useless or incorrect knowledge. Or they will not let go of the worldly thinking that keeps them from embracing Christ–like thinking. In such cases, spiritual maturity is not going to happen. No person can become a "new creature" unless he is willing to forsake the "old man" of sin that was buried in the water of baptism. Letting go of the "old self" and choosing to pursue "newness of life" is what it means to deny oneself (Mat. 16:24, Rom. 6:3–7, and 2 Cor. 5:17). Paul's own experience exemplifies this: he counted all things as "rubbish" in order to gain Christ. In other words, he let go of his old life (in Judaism) to cling to a new–found life in Christ (Phil. 3:7–8).

Nothing we have chosen to do or believe is worth keeping that threatens our relationship with God. Whatever you once chose to do, you can also *un*–choose it. For example, if you have chosen to use anger as a means of dealing with people who disagree with you, you can *un*–choose that reaction and choose a Christ–like one instead. Or if you have chosen to live in bitterness and victimhood because of some injustice against you, you can *un*–choose that mentality and live in peace and practice forgiveness instead. Or if you have tenaciously clung to some idea that remains unsupported by Scripture (and is unprofitable), you can *un*–choose that belief and fill your heart with that which comes from God instead.

You cannot "draw near to God" until you truly leave the world behind (James 4:8). You cannot "seek *first*" God's kingdom and righteousness until you make everything else in your life *second* to these (Mat. 6:33). You cannot "be transformed by the renewing of your mind" while remaining conformed to the thinking of this world (Rom. 12:2). You cannot "hold fast" to what is good until you "abstain from every form of evil" (1 Thess. 5:19–22). And you cannot "grow in the grace and knowledge" of Christ until you let go of the bitterness, selfishness, and false information of the world (2 Peter 3:18).

We must not become enslaved by our own opinions, attitudes, or behaviors. With the same power we exerted to *choose* to believe one way or another, so we can *un*–choose it, if indeed it opposes God's word. One thing *cannot* be "un–chosen," however: the decision to become a Christian in the first place. A person can be an unfaithful Christian, but he (or she) will still be held accountable to what he agreed to do when he was baptized. We cannot un-baptize anyone; we cannot make a person "un-born again"; and Christ cannot "un-circumcise" the heart (Col. 2:11–12). Since we are committed to Christ for life, it is in our best interest to yield to Him in every respect. In due time, He will complete and perfect us when we do so—which is exactly what we want (1 Peter 5:10).

Praying for One Another

Prayer is the key ingredient to spiritual health and success. The practice of prayer is necessary to conform to Jesus and achieve spiritual maturity. Along with study of God's word and Christian fellowship, prayer is indispensable for a healthy spiritual life. No soul will enter heaven that is not prayerful here on earth. Yet, it is not enough to pray for oneself; we must also pray for others. Through prayer, we help those who are also serving the Lord. As a result, our faith is strengthened, those for whom we pray receive divine help, and God is glorified.

The selfish person only caters to his own needs or is concerned only with his own struggles. Satan, through subtlety and deceit, often successfully distracts us from focusing on what is in our best interest and that of others. Because of this, Christians may become overwhelmed with the cares and worries of this world, making them ineffective at praying for others (or even themselves). Yet the gospel teaches that praying for "one another" (fellow believers) is a healthy and necessary function of the body of Christ. Jesus prayed for His disciples—and all *future* disciples—even as He faced imminent torture and death (John 17:1–26). While in his own literal imprisonment, Paul prayed for Christians everywhere. He knew that his personal circumstances could not hinder the activity or success of prayer (2 Tim. 2:9). So it is with us: no person or thing can prevent us from praying for one another.

Prayers for one another cannot be rare or sporadic but must be part of our lifestyle. We are to be "devoted" to prayer (Rom. 12:12, Col. 4:2). This requires the *intensity, urgency,* and *specificity* of prayer. ("Specificity" means: be specific for what you are asking, if possible.) In praying for one another, we partake in preserving the "unity of the Spirit" (Eph. 4:3) and unity with the brethren. If we are sincerely praying for one another, it makes it impossible for us to criticize, hold grudges, or become disconnected from one another. Through our mutual prayers, we recognize that we are a *family* that needs to show concern and take interest in each member *of* our family.

Jesus believed in prayer, as did Paul. On several occasions, Paul asked Christians to "pray for me (or us)" (Rom. 15:30, Eph. 6:18–19, 1 Thess. 5:25, and 2 Thess. 3:1). Paul credited the "prayers of many" for deliverance from his enemies and other problems (2 Cor. 1:10–11). This does not mean that prayer makes all our problems go away. God does not see tragedy, trials, persecution, disappointment, or even death in the same way we do. "Deliverance" might not be a rescue from one's present problems but being brought home to God.

We ought to give thanks to God for answering our prayers, regardless of *how* He does so or whether we agree with His answers. This may be difficult, but in doing so we defer to God's omniscience and perfect judgment over our own finite and limited perspective. Prayer works on a cause–and–effect basis, but is not the same as in the physical world. Prayer causes things to happen, but the effect is not always predictable, simply because of the staggering number of variables, the supernatural ability of God, and the fact that prayer is not an exact science with rigid formulas. While we do not know exactly *how* God will answer, we *do* know that His answer will always be in the best interest of the one for whom the prayer was asked.

We ought to consider the benefits to ourselves for having prayed for one another. First, it develops our faith in prayer, provided that we pray in faith. Praying without faith is like speaking without love (1 Cor. 13:1)—it is just noise and wasted effort. All earnest prayer begins with faith and is substantiated with fact. When we see prayers being answered—the "fact" part of prayer—it only increases our faith *in* prayer. Second, it develops an appreciation for God's ability to act. God is far greater and stronger than we imagine Him to be (Eph. 3:20–21). He in fact exceeds all human expectations—He exceeds our faith and thus the prayer *born* of human faith. Third, it develops our dependence upon Him versus reliance on our own efforts, the efforts of others, the ingenuity of man (doctors, technology, legal systems, etc.), or sheer luck. Human efforts or inventions cannot solve moral or spiritual problems. This does not mean that God will not *use* these things to help us or others but that He does not *have* to. Finally, it develops an accurate and real-world perspective for us. When we see fellow Christians suffering, we need not think that God has forgotten them. Instead, we realize that *despite* such temporary suffering, God is in control and "all things work together for good" (Rom. 8:28).

We are not really *commanded* to pray for one another as much as we are (as Christ's disciples) *expected* to do so. However, we cannot pray for anyone until we have examined our own heart. We cannot ask for God's divine gifts (such as mercy, grace, and deliverance) to be given to others if we ourselves have spurned them. Those with a pure heart and a fervent love of the brethren who actively pray for others are to be commended. Such people need to keep doing what they know to be right, and even "excel still more" (1 Thess. 4:1, 10).

Giving Thanks

According to the Law of Moses, Israelite men were designated with a special piece of clothing. In Num. 15:37–41, Israelite men were commanded to put blue tassels on the bottom fringe of their cloaks to publicly identify them as being holy to the Lord. Christians practice something similar today: whenever we bow our heads in a prayer of thanks before a meal, we are publicly identified as belonging to God. This practice is worthy of our discussion—not to dogmatize or formalize it, but simply to take an objective look at why we do this and how it should be done with a proper attitude.

First, what should we call this practice? Some call it "saying grace"— "grace" meaning an acknowledgment of the meal as a "gift" (and not God's saving grace). Yet, this expression is awkward and somewhat outdated. Some refer to it as "asking the blessing," as used in Mat. 26:26, but there are some misconceptions associated with this (discussed below). "Giving thanks" is the most common expression in Scripture for this practice. This phrase accurately describes what is being done and its purpose. Giving thanks is not literally commanded, but we have several examples of Jesus doing this prior to a meal (John 6:23), including the Lord's Supper. Likewise, Paul practiced this (Acts 27:35) and spoke of prayers with reference to food (Rom. 14:6, 1 Cor. 10:27–31). In the New Testament, giving thanks before a meal seems to be expected and customary among God's people.

There may be misconceptions about what is being done during the giving of thanks, however. Some act as though this prayer literally changes the food, as though it were "made sacred" or "made safe (to eat)." The blessing does nothing to the food; it is not *for* the food but is for the believer who takes time to acknowledge God as the provider *of* it. In other cases, well-intentioned Christians use the time to give thanks as an opportunity to sermonize and speak on several other subjects. This is not necessary and obscures the true intention or motive of the prayer in the first place. (But neither should the prayer be so short that it appears careless and disrespectful, as in, "Dear God, thanks for the food!—Amen.") Finally, the giving of thanks appears only to have been done (in New Testament examples) before meals. This means it is not necessary to do this for snacks, desserts, appetizers, etc.—although a person may choose to do so anyway at his own discretion. (Overdoing something good, however, *can* turn it into an empty formality or mindless tradition.) The intent of the prayer is to give thanks for another meal—whether that meal is leftovers or food which may not be our *favorite* choice to eat.

When giving thanks in public, we should be quiet, modest, and discreet. This is an excellent time to "let your light shine" in God's honor (Mat. 5:16). Doing this also emboldens us to do other difficult "good works" in public. We ought never to be embarrassed of this, however—what shame is there in giving God His due honor? Some onlookers will sneer, to be sure; others will respect us; still others may even question why *they* do not give thanks. If we are ridiculed for doing what is right, we have no need to fear; God is the One who justifies us, if we act properly and for the right reason (1 Cor. 4:3–4, 1 Peter 3:13–17). Considering this, we should never reduce the giving of thanks to the practice of a mere, mechanical ritual (as in, "Let's hurry up and give thanks so we can eat").

Giving thanks at the beginning of the meal sets the right context for what occurs *during* it. For example, how can a person give thanks, and then gossip through his meal, or speak evil of others, or engage in wickedness afterward? Public prayer forces us to live the life publicly that we have professed privately; by engaging in it, we admit that we are children of the kingdom, and not people of the world (Eph. 5:3–5). This sets us apart from others, just as the blue tassels set the men of Israel apart from men of other nations. Additionally, giving thanks for simple meals helps us to be thankful in other areas of our lives. When it is done properly, it teaches our children that God is holy, prayer time is a quiet and reverent experience, and when one member of the family prays aloud, the whole family solemnly participates *in* that prayer. (It is not "cute" if children act silly during prayer and their parents do nothing to correct this.) This practice also helps us to take our religion out of the church building and into everyday life, even when it is uncomfortable, inconvenient, and challenging.

Giving thanks ought never to be a dry, tedious, or thoughtless formality. Instead, we ought to look forward to giving thanks to our God, for He is certainly worthy *of* our thanks (Psalm 109:30). It also helps us to remain humble by reminding us that He is the source of *all* blessings. God wants to hear us pray, since prayer demonstrates our faith in His promises and our confidence in His ability.

❦END❧

Sources Used for This Study

Barnes, Albert. *Barnes' Notes* (electronic edition). Database © 2014 by WORDsearch Corp.

Crabb, Larry. *Inside Out.* Sisters, OR: Multnomah Press, 1988.

Crozier, Edwin. *Praying Like the Psalmists: A Study of the Psalms.* Temple Terrace, FL: Florida College Press, 2016.

Lenski, R. C. H. *Commentary on the New Testament* (vol. 8): *The Interpretation of St. Paul's Epistles to the Galatians, to the Ephesians, and to the Philippians.* Peabody, MA: Hendrickson Publishers, 1998.

Shirer, Priscilla. *Fervent.* Nashville, TN: B & H Publishing Group, 2015.

Sychtysz, Chad. *A Study of the Book of Psalms.* Waynesville, OH: Spiritbuilding Publishers, 2020.

_____. *Christian Thinking.* Waynesville, OH: Spiritbuilding Publishers, 2016.

_____. *Galatians and Ephesians Commentary.* Waynesville, OH: Spiritbuilding Publishers, 2024.

_____. *Seeking the Sacred.* Waynesville, OH: Spiritbuilding Publishers, 2009.

_____. *Titus and James Commentary.* Waynesville, OH: Spiritbuilding Publishers, 2024.

Ward, Nathan. *Our Eyes Are on You: A Biblical Study of Prayer.* Tampa, FL: DeWard Publishing Co., Ltd., 2023.

www.ingramcontent.com/pod-product-compliance
Lightning Source LLC
Chambersburg PA
CBHW042350040426
42449CB00018B/3477